Words Matter

A collection of vignettes examining the shared spaces of
motherhoood, marriage, friendship, aging, and femininity

by Judy Marano

DORRANCE
PUBLISHING CO
EST. 1920
PITTSBURGH, PENNSYLVANIA 15238

Dorrance Publishing Co
585 Alpha Drive
Suite 103
Pittsburgh, PA 15238
Visit our website at *www.dorrancebookstore.com*

ISBN: 978-1-6853-7121-0
eISBN: 978-1-6853-7966-7

Table of Contents

Foreword

There exists a uniformity in the human experience. When we strip away many of the external facets, at our core, the intrinsic truth is that humans desire to be loved, seen, and heard. We strive to receive this nourishment through our interactions within our microcosm of family, friends, colleagues, and strangers. One of the major "food groups" of this nourishment is the words we use and how we use them. Using my skills as an educator, mother, and coach, I hope to use my stories to inspire others to seek this spiritual and emotional nourishment and nourish those around them. I often remind my students to "change the words if you want to change the dynamic." We are all searching for a new, better version of ourselves but often don't know how to achieve it. It only takes a few minor changes and maybe a change of scenery to make that happen. Each of my meditations should allow for a pause for thought and provide a more straightforward path to the best version of yourself.

"Words Matter" is a phrase I often use with my students to show them that anything that comes out of their mouths carries weight. If more people took this saying to heart, there would be fewer personal, local, and even international misunderstandings. "Words are your superpower, and they must be used for good." I also tell them that once the sound passes your lips, there are no take-backs. So be careful!

When I began writing these short passages, I started with the idea of words. Unfortunately, words are haphazardly tossed around, or even worse, misused. I seek to find new definitions to redefine how we look at the world.

I was recently asked to classify my genre. Is it a memoir? Sort of. All the moments are genuine, so I guess they are part of my story. Maybe we can call it a self-help book. But for that to happen, we need to be looking for help. Sometimes we are just looking for a new perspective. The word mediation can seem scary. Many relate it to religion or yoga, but in my case, it does not matter what you believe. I hope you take these words and use them in a way that makes you feel your best. Dog-ear the passages that genuinely hit home so you can go back and reflect or share. Each is a small piece of my heart that I am so honored to share with you.

Judy

I'm OK: What Does That Really Mean for You?

Did you ever stop and think about how many times a day you use the word *Okay* or the even shorter version *OK*?

The word nerd inside me loves word history, and this little word's origin is filled with some fascinating lore. Some say the word comes from the Scottish, derived from "och aye" or from the Louisiana French, derived from "au Quai." My favorite story is that it was used after a battle in the Civil War to indicate zero killed. However, the word's actual story is a lot less interesting than the myths surrounding it. Yet as quickly debated as its origin is the meaning assigned to it. Since this is not a discussion on linguistics, I want to focus more on how everyone assigns it a different meaning.

Let's look at its everyday usage. You go to a movie and tell your friends the plotline is "OK." But what exactly does that mean to you? Did you like it? Would you recommend it? The term seems insufficient for the message that you want to send.

Or you recover from the flu, and you say that you are feeling OK. Does that mean you are ready to Climb Mount Kilimanjaro or tackle the grocery store? I can understand neither the intensity of your emotions nor the strength of your convictions here. In both examples, the word *OK* can have multiple definitions that could lead to a very different outcome if misunderstood.

In a world where communication is deteriorating daily, we put a lot of faith in a simple word. How can one word mean so many things to so many people? The Greeks were much better than most with their creation of language. They have a few words for the feeling of love because they clearly saw that love for pizza and love for your spouse are not the same thing. Maybe we need a plethora of words to express what these two tiny letters try to do.

I have thought about using and overusing this word a lot as I find myself using it as the default when someone asks how I am feeling since the onslaught of autoimmune diseases in my late thirties.

While many of the difficulties that I have faced have been those that impact my immune system, I am very cognizant that those who suffer from physical disabilities must also deal with the pity and prejudice from the abled-community whose version of OK is nothing like mine. Self-preservation. Mental health. The need for social cohesion. The desire to be viewed as strong and stable. These are some of my reasons for defaulting to OK.

I am reminded of a recent conversation with a coworker. I must have been having a terrible day because she asked if I felt all right. I said I was OK. But what I really wanted to say was that I had not been sleeping (thus the dark circles) because the weather change had triggered my inflammation and pain. She nodded kindly and went on about her most recent breakup. This was a clear reminder that in the minds of most, if you get up every day, go to work, and smile at your neighbors, you must be OK.

This is particularly true of family members. It makes my husband and kids feel better to know that I am doing fine. It means I can live up to their expectations of me as a wife and mom. There is comfort in knowing the woman of the house is steadfast and strong. It does not matter if you are a stay-at-home mom, a doctor, or the CEO of Google; you are expected to be the person responsible for your family's emotional health and well-being.

It feels like any demonstration of weakness would disrupt the pillars of the family unit and cause anxiety.

Recently, my mom and I went to work on my family's vacation home. We spent the weekend cleaning, laughing, and waiting for deliveries. Over the three days, my mom must have said, "You know I am almost eighty. I am tired" about twenty times. My mom, tired? No way. My response was the same every time. "Mom, you are not getting old. Stop complaining." A few days later, I was retelling this story to a friend who astutely pointed out that my denial of my mom's increasing age was to make me feel better. If I still saw her as young and energetic, there would be no way she was getting old. Even as an adult, the concept of not having my mom around is just too scary for me.

I am not advocating walking about all day spewing your aliments—could you imagine what a dismal life that would be if you said, "My day sucks, you?" This type of conversation is inherently toxic as it prevents you from relishing any points of joy you are having. And to be completely honest, American society encourages us to respond with niceties and templated responses. That is the underpinning of small talk.

Do these ideas encapsulate everyone's motivation? Absolutely not. Motivation is produced out of circumstance, and I only have my own to draw from. Others' pushes will be different.

I have recently decided that it is time to shake up my everyday conversations. Both of my children who live away from me now call every day just to check-in. Instead of the rote "OK" response, I have begun saying things like, "Tell me about your day" or "Guess what happened today?" Both statements serve as a jumping-off point to a more in-depth, more meaningful conversation. In addition to growing closer, I hope that as they grow older, they will realize that...

It is OK not to be OK.

Mindful Approach to Restoring Your Balance in Body, Mind, and Spirit

From our first steps, each memorable moment of our lives leads us to find our balance. As parents, we watch with bated breath as our child takes their first wobbly steps, and then we applaud and carry on as though they just landed on the moon. We repeat our excitement when we gift them the big two-wheeler on their seventh birthday and then tirelessly run behind the bike, screaming, "You got this!" as the child struggles to stay upright.

Children throw themselves with wild abandonment into learning to walk or ride that bike. For them, balance is a physical sensation; you either have it or keep trying until you get it.

If they fall, they do not go off, sulking their disappointment away. Instead, they jump right back up and try again.

As we age, the concept of balance takes on a different importance. We are told that as we reach our later years, we must continue to work on balance to stave off the falls that could lead to a multitude of other health issues, i.e., broken hips and fractured wrists. Luckily, I am not of the falling age yet, but I have been struggling with balance.

While practicing yoga, I tend to avoid the tree pose or any one-legged stance because inevitably, I can only hold the pose for about twenty seconds before falling to the side, windmilling my arms, fighting for recovery. But the harder I try to regain my balance, the more likely it is that I will fall—

possibly hurting myself or at least my ego. To rectify this, I decided that I needed to make a mental change: I needed to think like a child. That meant I needed determination, repetition, no fear of falling, all the while repeating the mantra "I've got this."

So today, after weeks of repetition, I was able to hold a tree pose successfully. What had changed?

With no one watching me, I was not afraid that I would fall and embarrass myself. I was not looking at other people and comparing myself to them. I was not afraid of the judgment that would be put upon me if I failed. Finally, I knew that I was "enough" and was not concerned about feeling "less than" in someone else's eyes. The world felt steady, so balance was achieved.

We are such a competitive species that we let other people's opinions of us undermine our self-worth.

It can be a real challenge to ignore what others say about us because we want to feel liked, admired, looked up to. But the words and actions that accomplish this are also the words that can destroy us.

Having balance means so much more than merely finding core stability and strength. Balance is not just an inner ear thing; it centers around the mind. Learning the lessons from my tree pose, I now need to apply them to my life. But balance in life is much more challenging than balance in yoga. How can I find the time needed to dedicate myself to self-improvement? What other issues must I push aside to allow for the repetition of positive actions? How can I get over the fear of falling both physically and emotionally? Who is going to be my person, screaming, "You got this!"

To tackle this daunting litany of questions, I started with the simple task of adding "me time" to my daily calendar. Whether it was a walk, yoga, or learning to speak a foreign language, I made it harder just to skip it when I included this time into my daily plan. It was now part of my day.

Next, I limited my time doing things that do not bring me joy. Yes, we have to clean, grocery shop, and pay bills, but I don't have to connect with a friend that drains me of my energy. I also do not have to make obligatory phone calls when a text check-in will do.

Finally, despite being an independent, self-reliant woman who doesn't want to rely on others to help me, the reality is, without outside assistance, none of us is likely to find what we are looking for. Fortunately, I have found my people. They are my tribe. There are only a few of them, but if it's cheering me on for my accomplishments or supporting me through my failures, I can depend on them to have my back. In exchange, I am available 24/7 as their support and sounding board.

When I think about balance, I now think about the push and pull of life that can easily land us on our asses if we are not paying attention.

To avoid this pitfall, the key is to make a plan that will move us closer to the balance we seek—and stick with it. We are not children who can fly by the seat of our pants anymore and live life as if we have no responsibilities. But with a few lifestyle changes, we can find that sweet spot where the ground is steady, and we feel in control. In other words, we can find balance.

The Box Theory

The theory of evolution. The string theory. The big bang theory. The theory of relativity. Although these scientific breakthroughs have altered the way we study life and our existence, I have a hard time seeing how they make my everyday life easier. On the other hand, my theory is not endorsed by any famous scientist; it comprises ideas I learned from psychologists, therapists, and some good old-fashioned soul searching. When I struggle with all the tasks of job, mother, wife, and life, I turn to the Box Theory.

Many of us, myself included, when faced with multiple challenges, become paralyzed to act. Despite our best efforts, we often internalize our problems until they become one giant inky Hydra-like monster. We know that one action will not address the stress of one million responsibilities, and sometimes we are afraid that committing to one course will lead us to fail in another. Even when we finally attempt to act, there is the question of which problem to attack first. That process, in and of itself, can cause me to give up and run for cover.

If what I am saying resonates with you, the next time you face this exact situation, stop and try this visualization activity: aka, The Box Theory.

Imagine your brain is a large storage facility lined with shelves waiting to be filled. You can get fancy and chose colors or stick with the metal industrial look. Now, think about all the stressors in your life. For each one, pick a box and create a significant label: work, health, family, or, more specifically, kids.

The kind of box you choose is a matter of style, but for me, the cardboard moving boxes that stack easiest are what I work with.

Now the hard part.

As you take your first morning inhale at the beginning of the day, quickly scan through the activities and emotions you need to access. My list looks something like this: arthritis pain, frustrations, school, students, children, husband, volunteerism, etc. I then picture myself taking each of these issues and placing them into the appropriately labeled box. I then cover and file each box on a shelf—higher shelves for things that can wait and lower shelves for the ones I might need sooner.

The official name for this activity is compartmentalizing, put everything in place, and handle them one at a time. Neither therapists nor I advocate shoving ideas in sealed boxes and hoping they disappear. They do not. But this strategy can be used to help us access issues when we need them and not feel overwhelmed.

Once you've seen and placed each item on the proper shelves, then breathe.

You have, within the span of a few minutes, organized your life into a series of small containers. Think of it as straightening your desk before the workday. I know I am much more productive when my space is clean. The tricky part is not to poke around once the box is closed. You need to let go of the object, stress, or aggravation because you have put it just out of reach. Sometimes there is comfort in knowing the problem will not dictate how you spend your day. On the other hand, if new stressors arise, you have space and the ability to deal with them immediately.

I can imagine many of you rolling your eyes or thinking this will not work for you. You would not be the first to dismiss this idea as the ramblings of a crazy mind.

You probably think that you can just ignore these thoughts and pressures and move through your day. While that may seem like an excellent solution, ignoring ideas does not make them go away. They are in your brain, waiting to pop up during a moment of weakness when you let your guard down. But let me assure you, there is evidence that when done correctly, you can achieve a clearer mind and start your day prepared to take on the world.

I have explained this strategy to several people who look at me like I might be crazy. But it has allowed me to find a peaceful mind. Now I have to say; this plan did not work after the first or second, or even third try. I could do the visualization part, but I originally had a hard time sticking to my guns and not revisiting the boxes.

Today, I am a huge proponent of this theory, and I can honestly say that I have mastered it with practice. Now at the start of every day, I can wake up and begin my daily evaluation. I might start with, "My arthritis is feeling terrible today."

Instead of dwelling on it and giving the discomfort the power to control and determine how the day will play out, I say, "No, you are going away for a while. I will check on you again at the end of the day." Problem solved. I can start my day clear-minded until 3:00 p.m. when I can pay attention to the issue that I have shelved.

The Importance of Community Service in Shaping the Values of Our Children

As parents negotiating our small children's lives, many often seek information on not screwing up our kids. We tap into the wisdom of more experienced adults who have lived through the trials of raising young humans in this complicated world and have come out on the other side with well-adjusted adults.

It was not surprising when a young father recently asked me for the "magic trick" to turn his children into children resembling my two sons.

This young father, who has known my boys since they were small, has often remarked how impressed he is with their maturity and moral compass.

I am not sure what he was expecting because I would be a wealthy woman if I answered that question. But I assume he was expecting standard solutions like "stress structure," "allow time for creative play," and "teach manners and responsibility." Although I believe each of these skills will indeed assist in any young person's growth and maturity, my response of "Get involved in community service" had him furrowing his brow with a look of skepticism. No magic here.

After a few moments, I continued, "The most important thing my husband and I did was to make community service a priority in your boys' lives."

I am not saying that we wanted to expose our children to those who have less than them to make them grateful, like the people who say, "finish your food because children are starving in Africa." First of all, expressing this to children will probably not be well understood; it also fosters the idea that service is punishment for "rotten" behavior. Secondly, that mindset is highly abusive and manipulative to those you are helping; those who need assistance aren't your teaching tools—they are people humbly asking for help.

My children are the direct descendants of a family of "doers." When we first moved to our small suburban town, my husband sought out an organization where he could donate his time. The local ELK's Lodge provided him with an opportunity to raise money and awareness for charities and also build a network of friends. As soon as the boys were old enough, we would serve cake and juice at the senior citizen picnics. The kids loved the attention from the elderly, who saw them as the adorable kids they were. It didn't hurt that many picnickers would give them quarters or dollars as a thank you.

From there, we tried the same approach with an organization helping the disabled. Maybe this one was not as "fun," but it did help my healthy boys to see that not everyone is the same. We never had to tell them to be kind to others despite their differences because, for them, everyone who was kind to them received kindness in return.

And if they faced a person who wasn't helpful or giving, we just reminded them that sometimes people have pain that you can't see.

I don't want you to think we only introduced our kids to the harsh realities of life, aging, and disabilities because they also spent many a Christmas season selling Christmas trees for charity. I can still see their smiling faces as our two little guys, bundled in snowsuits, helped to drag a six-foot tree to the car of a waiting family.

Years later, without much persuasion, they still love the idea of bringing Christmas joy to people. They introduced their girlfriends to the practice this year, neither of whom has ever done anything like this. Their joy was so palpable that I think this might become a new part of our family's Thanksgiving traditions.

These unselfish lessons have taught my sons humility. They have incredible respect for the elderly and understand that it only takes a few moments to change someone's day. They also learned that different is not less. To this day, my boys are the ones offering a hand or support to anyone who needs it. However, the most important lesson they learned was that they are fortunate for their family, home, and health, things that are not to be taken for granted.

We all have continued doing service, both in our communities and work environments. For example, one of my sons was recently tasked by his company to organize a fundraiser for Make a Wish. The other son regularly gives blood (he says he HAS to do it every eight weeks because "if I don't do it, I can't expect others to help me when I need it") and participates in Operation Christmas Child to collect boxes of presents to send to orphanages.

I am currently involved in many projects to better my community, and I often speak to groups of college students about the need for service. Their immediate response is always, "I don't have the time." There are just no more hours to give between job, family, school, and life, but inevitably, once I start talking about the success stories and the very personal impact we have had on others' lives, these students can't wait to jump in. When you find something that you can devote X hours a week doing, you will be amazed by how the time makes itself available.

Community service has cognitive, social, and physiological benefits.

It is an integral part of religious traditions stretching back for centuries. There is a common thread through all religions (Jewish, Sikh, Hindu, Christian, etc.) that service is the way to a more vibrant, fulfilling spiritual life. In a recent study from the University of Nevada Reno, Molly Latham found that teens say the benefits received from volunteering include:

- Learning to respect others
- Learning to be helpful and kind
- Learning to understand people who are different
- Developing leadership skills
- Becoming more patient
- Acquiring a better understanding of citizenship

Service helps both the giver and receiver; this is not a new idea. The recently passed Ram Dass, a psychology professor-turned-spiritual teacher, explains this beautifully:

"Helping out is not some special skill. It is not the domain of rare individuals. It is not confined to a single part of our lives. We heed the call of that natural impulse within and follow it where it leads us."

But to be clear, service is not something you should do because you want accolades. Without a doubt, much good comes from putting yourself second for a few moments, but for me, the reason to get my family involved in service is that my children are good human beings. And let's be honest, isn't that what we want most for our children?

As Martin Luther King Jr. aptly said, "Darkness cannot drive out darkness; only light can do that.... Haters cannot drive out hate; only love can do that." We need to show our children how to be that light that will lead to a brighter future.

---

1 https://www.psychologytoday.com/us/blog/cui-bono/201305/selfless-service-part-i-is-selfless-service-possible

2 https://www.unce.unr.edu/publications/files/cd/2003/fs0323.pdf

3 https://www.huffpost.com/entry/giving-back-how-you-and-t_n_832401

NO! - An Underused Word

Examining our character flaws can be daunting. There are so many parts of us that we want to change or improve upon. For me, the biggest challenge is my inability to say "NO." And I think that I am not the only one.

I enjoy the joy that I can bring to others by watching their dog or running an errand or even helping them find a job. For me, the ability to make someone's life a bit easier is the equivalent of receiving a present or cooking a meal for a group of friends. It gives me that warm, satisfied feeling. I would define myself as a people pleaser. The reality is, there is a scientific reason that I feel like this. Giving sends a small burst of dopamine to my brain, reaffirming that I am doing something right. This is similar to the burst of happiness you feel after running a mile or getting a hug. Overall, that is not a negative character trait, but as with any addiction, too much of a good thing can be draining on the mind and harmful to the body.

Recently, I was feeling the physical exhaustion of taking on the world's problems and needs, and I had to stop and question why I seemed to have an inability to say "no" when asked to help someone. I have even gone so far as to convince myself that my saying "yes" is actually what I want and, therefore, it would make me happy. Why can't I say "no"?

No. It's a simple word, yet we have assigned it a compelling message. Particularly in Generation X, we were brought up on the idea that "busy was ideal." Look busy, and the rest of the world will know that you are a competent, helpful, resourceful person. Rest, and you are lazy. So, saying no is reinforcing the characterization that I am selfish and lazy. Neither of those things is true.

That is the view from the outside in, but the inside out view is just as damaging. In this cutthroat, get-ahead environment, we are afraid of what impression we are giving off by not doing something we are asked to do. If I say no to a job project, will that jeopardize my ability to get a promotion? If I say no to my husband, will he seek a woman who would be more accommodating?

These thoughts are one of the main reasons why many of us are pushing ourselves to be all things to all people. Fear is a powerful motivator, and it is this fear that prevents us from upsetting the apple cart.

The reality is that saying no to a spouse is not sending you to divorce court, just like saying no to your boss is not putting you on the unemployment line. This begs the question, why is it so hard?

Of course, I can refer back to the people pleaser, but I think there is more to this. I spent about two hours to and from the airport with a past student. He was struggling to figure out his life path after a stint in the armed forces. On our first trip, we brainstormed motivations and possible paths he could take. While driving home, he announced that he had decided to be a fireman. He went on to explain that after many hours soul-searching, he realized that he "needed" to do a job where he "could save someone's life." He continued explaining that each action or success in the military was followed by an emotional upswing that would carry him until the next event. He wanted that feeling again. His words were like a shining light on my dilemma. If you are not helping people, it is a limitation to personal growth. The only way to get that "high" is to do something tangible. My saying "yes" and possibly changing someone's life trajectory is what I need to hold me until the next available opportunity.

This is the essence of the problem. We need to figure out a way to find the balance between doing for others and doing for ourselves. Listen to your body and think about if saying yes will negatively impact your mental or physical well-being.

Once that is done, we need to practice without feeling obligated to apologize for our decision. It doesn't count if you say "no" and follow it with what you feel is an acceptable excuse. "No, I can't go to the party. My child has the flu." Just say, "No, thank you." Start with the small stuff. Things like, "no, I would not like another helping of pie." Or "no, I cannot grab the phone." Then, move to the bigger stuff. Be confident that your one "no" will not undermine your womanhood, marriage, or job. What it will do is show that you are strong, confident, and know your abilities. The next time you say "yes," you will know that it is something you want to do, and your "yes" will be more meaningful because it's coming from a place of genuine care and desire rather than obligation.

Time to Clean Your House

When we reach adulthood, we are obligated to undertake certain things—keeping your house running, keeping your car running, and keeping yourself healthy. These skills are often passed on from the domestic leading parent regardless of sex. They are the trifecta of adulthood.

My mom used to clean the refrigerator out each week before the Friday night family grocery shop. I clearly remember her standing in front of the open fridge, repeating her mantra, "When in doubt, throw it out." Bags of unrecognizable food were tossed in the trash. Then we would clean the shelves in preparation for the latest round of food for the week. Before long, I recall these exact words when cleaning out the unworn clothes or the closet full of junk. I can see my mom going into my teenage room, dumping my drawers out to ferret through the too-small items and making order out of the remaining wardrobe. I also recall not enjoying the process very much.

Flash forward 40 years.

After the long winter, my husband and I embarked on the basement cleanout. This entailed four to five hours going into the basement and food pantry's dark crevices and eliminating all superfluous things. I always start with the same mindset—dread, frustration, exhaustion, but I enjoyed myself after a few grueling hours this year. I loved the purge. I relished the large pile of garbage accumulating in the driveway. The odor rising from my newly bleached floor smelled like an accomplishment. Wait! What is wrong with me? Had some of my mom rubbed off on me?

First, I was scared that I was enjoying cleaning. Did that mean I was succumbing to the traditional gender roles of years gone by? What was next? Ironing? NO! Of course, I needed to figure out why this change had occurred. Why was a cleaning, which used to be so painful, suddenly enjoyable?

I quickly determined with immense relief that it was not the process itself but the sense of accomplishment that clearing out the old and unneeded brought. It is the finding of an organization in chaos.

Suppose I can find happiness in my piles of debris literally and figuratively; what if I went through the same process with my brain? Am I storing useless information that is contributing to chaos? What am I holding on to, which is taking up space for something better?

Am I holding on to bad memories as a reminder to judge people unfairly? Research shows that I am not alone. Since emotions trigger our memories, the negative ones serve as reminders of things that caused us pain, not to repeat the actions.

"Memories are generally prone to distortion over time, but researchers have found some evidence to suggest that emotional memories are more resistant to the decay processes that wear away at all memories with time," says author Elizabeth Kensinger of Boston College. Not only are emotional memories harder to get rid of, but researchers have also shown that reliving these emotional memories reinforces negative emotions, which muddles the efficacy of the memory. Our brain will alter memories, and the recollection will no longer be precisely what happened. Everyone deserves a clean slate, and we cannot do that if we rely on manipulated memories to stereotype others. The only one hurt by holding grudges are the person doing the holding. The other person probably has moved on and is not dwelling on past interactions. As Alexander Pope once wrote, "To forgive is divine. "Make peace with your past and let go of the moments that bring you pain.

So, my foray into why cleaning made me so happy is a statement of my need to put things into their place. We have no problem finding chaos. Turn on the news, read the paper, talk to your kids. Many instances make us feel like that cluttered basement. We hold on to trash and life memories; they are lifeboats because the unknown is still scarier than repeating the past's pain. But the reality is that they are not saving us; they are the anchors holding us back. They are the items that are in the way of clearing out our own houses. Think how wonderful you will feel when staring at the imaginary pile of trash and memories crowding up your space. Take the proverbial broom and clean the house. You will have an instant feeling of satisfaction and lightness.

Worry vs. Mindfulness: A Life Lesson

Last summer, my son and I decided to get matching tattoos. He was heading to graduate school ten hours away, and I was having some trouble with the distance. So instead of sharing in his excitement for the challenges and opportunities ahead of him, all I could focus on were all the possible things that could go wrong that I could not fix from afar.

I would not consider myself a control freak but would definitely consent to being a type-A personality. I like to know what has, is, and will happen to those that I love. So, I guess you could say I like to be in control, which technically would make me a control freak (which is incredibly hard to admit).

He was tasked to pick both the symbol and design that we tattooed on our wrists—a symbolic sign of unity, so to speak. The symbol he chose was the Farsi calligraphy for This too shall pass. My son, a deeply spiritual young man, convinced me to get this image by explaining the meaning behind the saying.

Apparently, a king wanted to get a ring inscribed with words that would be meaningful for every moment of his life. One of his servants came back with the phrase, "this too shall pass." The king was thrilled because he could encompass the fluidity of life in this one simple quote.

Being a wise man, he knew that the secret to a happy life is to accept the pain because it is transient and relish the pleasure because that too will end.

For me, these words were perfect. They seemed appropriate for our situation, and their meaning gave me a sense of calm, albeit temporarily.

Unfortunately, a leopard cannot change its spots, and a mother cannot change her ways. As much as I tried, my need to control what came before and what will come later is encompassed in an all-too-familiar word: *worry*.

We all worry about daily aggravations, but my mother has mastered the art of worrying and has very graciously handed this down to me; I have made worrying an Olympic sport. Even when there are not things to worry about, I can create things. I can lose an entire night's sleep on the what-ifs or maybes.

I remember being told that worrying is the most useless emotion we can have. We are spending a lot of energy trying to control things that will end up precisely the way they were meant to be.

But once my brain starts going down this rabbit hole, there is no way to know just how far my negative thoughts will spin. Not the most helpful life tool.

Many years of therapy and soul searching have made me realize that there is an interesting dichotomy between the word *worry* and the now popular term *mindfulness*. Magazine articles, talk shows, and therapists around the globe encourage us to seek mindfulness. But do we really know what that word means and how to find it?

Here is a simple way to look at it: Worry involves fretting about things that we can't control, while Mindfulness is about awareness, and with that, an acceptance of the world that we live in. Obviously, these two emotions cannot coexist.

If I just stopped worrying about what might happen, maybe the result would be that I could live in the moment. But this is a significant change for me as I live to worry.

My big challenge is to push aside worry and to seek mindfulness daily. Although this change has taken a little time, what I do now is take each moment and say, "Do I have the power to change it?" The majority of the time, the answer is a resounding, "No." As much as I want to control the outcome, that is just not part of my skillset. The more I "let it go," the more I became aware of what is within my power to change.

That is what I think mindfulness means. It is enjoying the moments we have been given, possibly turning our backs on this digital world with information coming at us every three or four seconds on YouTube, the internet, and our watches. Whether you're a worrier like me or someone being held captive by technology, so many of us have stopped living in the moment. I think therein lies the value of mindfulness.

Ironically, while I was fighting my demons of worry, I accidentally found the key to mindfulness. I am far from perfect, as I occasionally still slip into worry mode, but a simple glance down to my wrist reminds me what a brilliant king before already knew.

If I just hang on for a minute, this too shall pass....

Finding Solace in Silence

We live in a world of constant noise. From young children to the elderly, we listen to a podcast or watch a video, if it is not the TV or music. I used to convince myself that I needed "white noise" to be productive. I told myself that I just worked better in noise. Even as a young mother, I convinced myself that I should have the TV on for my kids to pick up new words and learn. Maybe that was partly true, but what was probably more real was that... I was afraid of silence, fearful of where my mind would travel left on its own.

So, for years, I filled my moments with noise. And believe me when I say there are plenty of sounds to be found—I threw myself into my children's school activities and afterschool sports. I organized fundraisers and even joined a group to revitalize an old theater—anything to keep me from the quiet. I thought all that noise insulated me from me. Avoiding silence became my superpower. The saying "ask a busy person if you want to get something done" became my mantra. I could be that busy person and appear to be all things for all people.

But I was hiding this deep dark secret. I hated silence.

Battling depression and anxiety, I tried to stay out of my head as much as possible. I saw a situation and automatically went to the worst possible outcome. If my husband was a few minutes late, I was sure there had been an accident. If my son forgot to text, I would call immediately to see if he was all right. I came to believe that this was just the way most people's (mother's) minds worked.

Boy, I was surprised when I was told that this was my anxiety speaking and my need to control everything to ensure everyone was safe and happy.

As my therapist told me, "Consider your head a bad neighborhood that should not be gone into alone or unprepared."

Now that my kids are grown and starting their own lives, I spend a good deal of time alone. Of course, I have my teaching, writing, and family to fill the void, but I have recently started investigating what would happen if I sought silence.

The first experience caught me by surprise when I was walking along the reservoir with a friend. We usually fill our walks with friendly banter on anything from local gossip to politics. But that day was different. We were both in contemplative moods and walked side by side, not saying a word. I started to hear things that I never had before. The thumping of our feet in unison as they hit the pavement, a bird chirping in the distance, the rumbling breeze picking up strength as it pushed through the trees.

How had I missed this? The sound of nature, life, movement. I was working so hard to avoid the silence that I was missing all that could be found within it. Instead of feeling fear, I felt like a wave of peace wash over me.

I am not going to say that I am cured of my fear of silence, but I am trying to overcome it, a little at a time. And it appears the Universe is on board. Days after my first eye-opening encounter, the storm knocked out our internet, cable, and lights. My initial reaction was panic, but I heard things I had never noticed before as I made my way around the house. The thump of the wet towels in the dryer and the branches against the roofline was almost musical. The sigh from my dog curled at my feet was pure love. In my silence, I found that the world is filled with the rhythms of life, things that should not be feared.

Nothing terrible happened while the power was out. My family remained safe without me calling them, and the sun went down without my help. In the silence, I found a new piece of my mind was awoken. Little by little, I began to tiptoe into that internal neighborhood I had avoided for so long, and to my surprise, instead of expecting darkness, it was a beautiful place filled with love, hope, and forgiveness.

Don't Tell Me You're Sorry: A Call for More Honest Communication

I feel like my grandmother when I start a sentence with "Back in the day...." But I think it is appropriate in this one case. So...

Back in the days when I was growing up, when a person said those two magic words—"I'm sorry"—it held an almost revered meaning. Most of the time, the words were accompanied by a grand gesture, a comforting touch, a solid shoulder to cry on, or a parent saying you should be. But as I have aged, that no longer seems to be the case.

Social situations and peers have dictated that those sentimental feelings should be pushed aside as they do not have a place in the grown-up world.

Now, "I'm sorry" has become a standard placeholder for a more valued phrase when you are attempting to placate another.

Recently, while on the phone with the insurance company (feel free to add any service industry that is more appropriate for your life) for a total of one hour, I was rewarded by a person jumping on the line every 6–7 minutes to tell me how sorry they were for the delay. Since I was multitasking, I heard the words but did not pay them much mind. But as time grew longer, I found myself getting more and more irritated by the seemingly meaningless words. Finally, at my breaking point when the woman said, "I'm sorry for the delay." I responded with, "No, I don't think you are." Suddenly there was silence on the other side of the phone. Had no one ever questioned her sincerity before because she certainly was taken aback? I sense that one of their scripts unempathetically read, "Tell the client you are sorry."

Although I wanted to explain my feelings, I felt that they would fall on deaf ears. But I did begin to think about when the words *I'm sorry* became the universal excuse/catch-all whenever you wanted absolution. The actual definition of the phrase means "Beg your pardon" or "Forgive me," and neither of these is a substitute for how we use the word.

It is incredible that when you stop and really listen to people, you notice how often they apologize for things they have no control over. My students often say, "I'm sorry I got that wrong." What they should be saying is, "I feel bad that I let you down," or "I don't know, and it embarrasses me."

The truth is, taking responsibility for our mistakes is much more complex than just asking for forgiveness. You are admitting that you are flawed, and in some way, that diminishes the shiny outside you show the world.

Other times I hear people apologizing for things like the weather ("I'm sorry you're cold") or even your mood ("I'm sorry you feel sad today"). Maybe it is their way of showing empathy, but it comes out more like a platitude since any overused word inevitably loses its power. Each time we apologize, we say I am responsible for the pain I have caused you, and I would like you to forgive me. But are you really responsible for someone else's physical or emotional well-being? No.

I was having a conversation with a friend about this topic, and she had an interesting approach. She told me that her "issue" was people arriving late to a meeting and saying they are sorry. How can two words rectify wasting busy people's time? How arrogant of the late person to think they are important enough to wait for. A better comment upon entering a room late would be, "Thank you for your patience." The simple rephrasing allows you to acknowledge your lateness. while at the same time recognizing that the people waiting for you deserve respect.

When we teach children their first words, we also express the meaning that the words should have. I think we can learn so much from these young minds. When my son was little, and he did something that either he knew was wrong or that we taught him was wrong, he would bow his head and say, "My sorry." It was the most endearing statement because not only was he feeling remorse, but he realized that saying those words was equivalent to giving a small piece of his heart. "My sorry" is giving some part of me, and hoping you will be open enough to receive and cherish it. Unfortunately, as he grew older, "My sorry" turned into "I'm sorry," a change that lost some of its personal appeal and meaning.

Here are some other ways to rephrase your thoughts:

Instead of "I'm sorry you are stressed," say, "Would you like me to help?"

Instead of "I am sorry to bother you," say, "I was hoping you could help me with something."

Instead of saying, "I am sorry that you are sad," say, "I am concerned about you."

Given how easy it is to toss off this oft-used phrase, what is the right way to say, "I'm sorry"?

My husband is like many men who guard their feelings and are reticent to express their emotions. But if my husband says he is sorry, he does it while looking into my eyes, and I can feel it in my soul. You see, if you treasure the words and only use them when they are appropriate, their meaning is so much greater.

The Complex Rules for Raising Adult Children: From Protector to Guide

Ask me how to take care of children. I got you. Ask me how to raise good people with manners. A mix of structure and praise does the trick. But ask me how to be the mother of two grown young men. I am clueless.

About a million books tell you how to raise your child, but the shelves are almost empty when looking for the Guide to a Relationship with Your Adult Children. Because let's face it, you have already instilled in them all the lessons you can. Before they aged out, they would listen (even if they pretended not to) when you talked about life and obstacles to avoid. Now, they claim to have the answers. Your one job was to protect them until they could protect themselves. It is biological. Once an animal can hunt or fly on its own, it doesn't need its mother for survival. While it seems so straightforward with animals, how do we change the dynamic from protection to one of guiding?

I must admit that these ideas only became relevant as I found myself messing up regularly with my young adult sons. Inevitably, they would snap back at a comment I made and respond with something like, "Mom, I don't need you to tell me that. I am an adult." This followed by me feeling bad that I hurt their feelings and insulted their maturity.

Ugh! How am I supposed to take twenty-four years of behavior and change it on the dime? The tricky part of this transition is that my blooming adults are trying to get their footing. Like a baby who has just learned how to walk, they run as fast and as far as they can away from mom, but the minute they falter, they come running back for help. Only to push away again. Fortunately, it gets better after college when they find their stride. Then the problem is less of a "them" problem and more a "me" problem.

So, after much reading, talking, and listening, I think I have narrowed down the three most important aspects of raising an adult.

These growing humans want to be seen, heard, and respected.

Let Them Be Seen

The fact is, our children are always going to be our babies, even when they are old and grey. But we need to see them as people. An excellent way to do this is to have a conversation about their likes and dislikes as if you were meeting for the first time. We accept new strangers into our fold regularly, so reintroduce yourself to this new version of your child. Find common ground. Figure out the activities you can partake in that are new. Try not to repeat the same stuff you did when they were children because you will fall into the motherly role again. For example, my son took a liking to country music as he searched for genres that fit who he is now. So that apparent common ground was a concert and dinner as adults. We laughed and shared stories like two old friends.

Most importantly, when a new friend reaches out or shows concern for you, you say thank you. Try thanking your child for calling or for meeting you for dinner. Change the dynamic, change the outcome.

Let Them Be Heard

Our rising adults are searching for the person they will be for the rest of their lives, and in doing that, they need to take what they learned as children, keep what fits, but also find new outlets.

They are formulating ideas and values that may differ from the ones you have.

Remember that you have instilled in them values that have been reinforced since birth. Do not think they will turn a blind eye and suddenly become someone you are afraid of. They remember. But political, social, and religious values change. The key here is to listen with an open heart and mind. DO NOT express a judgment. That is a surefire way to shut down the conversation. Instead, ask questions about their ideas and show them you appreciate their sharing. For me, this was a lesson in religious beliefs.

My children were brought up Catholic, as were my and my husband's families going back generations, long before they even set foot in America. So, when one of my sons announced that he would be a Protestant, my initial feeling was one of failure. But then I heard his reason: he felt that the church did not accept his drive to study science, specifically genetics, genetic engineering, and evolution; he also felt that the Catholic church did not support many of the social policies he felt strongly about, like feminism. Additionally, he spoke about how his faith reignited from the love, sense of belonging, and the social outreach of his new church. He found a church where he said, "I feel like I belong, and they love me for me." He found his fit and found the people who would help him grow into the man he dreamed of being.

Well, I could have stomped my feet and said that he was turning his back on tradition. But hearing the joy in him and seeing how he has been further transformed into a more confident and kinder man, I realized that the instinct to argue was not one of protection but rather self-preservation. I was initially so hung up on my sense of failure that I didn't want to hear him. But when I did, I was filled with a great sense of ease and pride that he has found his place. Now we often talk about his deepening faith, and it brings me joy that he has found a supportive, loving group of people with a similar value system.

Finally, Respect Them

We are used to being in charge and guiding decisions. Now we need to loosen the reins and let them make decisions on their own. Trust that they know what they are doing. As long as they are not hurting themselves or others, it is OK that things don't work out exactly as planned.

Let them succeed on their own. Let them fail knowing that you will be there to offer that new guidance when requested.

If that seems like letting go too fast, start by being the safety net under a trapeze artist. It is always there but never intrusive; sometimes, it is never seen by the audience. But if tragedy strikes, the net is there to catch the performer. Eventually, the trapeze artist will rarely, if ever, need the net—that is, until they introduce some new performers of their own.

This is so critical that the absence of respect, or perceived respect, can leave a person feeling restrained and infantilized. Something so simple as a family getaway can turn into a battle of wills if you insist on telling them what and how to arrange their plans. I made that mistake and tried to micromanage my rising adult. The result was a battle of wills and hurt words. A better way to handle it would have been to say, "You know how busy you are at work, figure out how much time you can give us. Anytime you can will be wonderful." Again, change the words, change the results.

The bumpy road from protector to guide can be difficult. But there are ways to navigate the process so that no feelings get hurt and everyone feels seen, heard, and respected. You can and should have a healthy relationship with your adult children and their new families as they grow and create their own families. I, for one, am excited about the people my children are becoming and the fact that we are slowly finding our new normal. If I need a subtle reminder, I look at my relationship with my mom, knowing that we, too, managed the transition from protector to guide to a friend. But that may be another story.

I Can't... or Maybe I Can: Releasing Our Limiting Beliefs of Our Potential

We've all been there. You are standing in the yoga or fitness class of your choice, preparing for an hour-long break in your routine. The instructor starts with some basic breathing, maybe a sun salutation. You are feeling good. You move to some more challenging poses (warrior two, side angle, etc.). So far, you are sure you are in a suitable class at the correct level. Then, the instructor describes something called a flying pigeon pose. It doesn't sound too crazy until she demonstrates it... Nope. I can't do that!

Maybe the "I can't" is just a reflex we fall back on when faced with a challenge. But as my mother always said, "If you don't try, how do you know you can't?" Sure, that works for trying spinach or riding a bike when you're nine....

But now the notion of "I can't" has taken on a completely different definition: fear of failure.

As a species, we are afraid of failure. No one wants to try something and fail at it because with failure comes embarrassment and shame.

I am brought back to when I was a child. The playground was what everyone waited for each day, but I was not the kickball kind of girl. I was the shy girl who sometimes got bullied, and I feared giving those bullies something to use against me. Instead of facing the criticism of my peers, I would regularly say, "I can't!" followed by some lame excuse like a headache, an injury, or even make up something more dramatic like my mom wouldn't want me to get all dirty.

The reality is that I was sure I was not good enough, so I spared myself the emotional trauma of failing by not trying.

Unfortunately, this fear of failure pokes its head out even into our adulthood. The situations are much more significant than playground games, but the emotions are the same. Your boss asks you to take the lead on a presentation. You know you are capable, yet you respond with, "I can't; I'm just too busy with X to take the time needed to give it my all." On the surface, you come across as a dedicated, focused worker that will make any boss feel proud, but you know that is not the case.

Failing in front of your coworkers would just be too humiliating. It is easier to preserve your dignity and make an excuse rather than risking failure.

How did we become so fearful? Where did the wild abandon of childhood go? Yes, we would get nervous at a dance recital or jumping into a pool to the waiting arms of a parent, but... we did not let that fear stop us from our accomplishments.

What happened to all the risk-takers of the world? Without these trailblazers, where would we be? People like Marie Curie or Sally Ride did not let the fear of failure stand in the way of progress or innovation. As women, they didn't allow a society that systematically questioned their ability to stop them. Because failure was just the next step to something greater and stopping where they stood would stop not only themselves but also young women who might follow in their footsteps.

Although many say the next generation is lazy and unmotivated, I do not see that. My son sent a text this morning that said, "Hey, Mom, I got 300 lbs. on the bench today." I know if I asked him two years ago to lift 300 lbs., he would have said, "I can't." Yet here he is, bigger and stronger. He took all his misses and failures, and instead of giving up, he pushed incrementally until he achieved his goal. There are plenty of excuses, like starting a career and achieving his goals. There are plenty of reasons for not doing something, for example, working fifty-hour weeks, social and business obligations. Still, he serves as an example that anyone can find the time to improve. We can learn from our children and their desire to see more of the world than what is right in front of them.

As I see it, the problem is we are bombarded by celebrities who look perfect, executives who excel in businesses, and philanthropists who work to save the world. They seem to make it look so easy, which creates a lot of pressure for the average Joe.

It's no wonder we are feeling inadequate when the bar has been set so high. But if you spoke with these same people, I doubt their rise to power and prestige was without failure. The biography of Michelle Obama tells the story of a girl who was not handed the silver ring, yet she managed to use what she was given to get the job done. Is she that different than any of us?

We need to put aside our desire to be perfect because it stands in the way of our progress. So what if we are not perfect at kickball or fall on our butt during yoga, or stutter during a presentation? We are capable of more than we allow ourselves to be. We need to turn our backs on being the best and listen to what Maya Angelou said: "You alone are enough. You have nothing to prove to anybody."

Reach for the stars or the moon and scream at the top of your lungs, "I can!" You might be pleasantly surprised to realize that you have been the greatest obstacle to your growth all along.

Wait for it: Exploring the Virtues of Patience

On a bitter 23 degrees morning, my walking partner and I set out on our daily constitutional walk along the reservoir. As we crossed the bridge over the frozen water, I saw a man quietly sitting on a chair on the ice, holding a 12-inch rod with line disappearing into a tiny hole.

Cupping my hands around my frozen lips, I yelled, "Did you catch anything?" He smiled and walked towards us so that we could talk. He was a cheerful man who told us he had been ice fishing for the past thirty years. He said it was his favorite time of the year. I am sure my face showed the skepticism I was feeling.

As I looked around the water, there was space that looked wet, definitely too thin to walk on. So, I asked, "How do you know the ice is safe?" He smiled as if he had heard this question once or twice and said he tests it and stays away from questionable areas. He went on to talk about the insulated suit that keeps him warm and dry while flashing his crampon and this ice claws hanging about his neck, "Just in case."

He then explained that he ice fishes to fill his freezer for the year. Apparently, freshwater fish taste entirely different coming from cold water. His summertime fishing was just for fun.

After waving goodbye, we continued our walk, and he resumed his sitting and waiting. I couldn't get him out of my mind. I used to fish and loved it when I was young, but that was on a warm summer day. The idea of sitting for hours in the cold waiting for a fish seemed ridiculous. No, thank you.

I had to laugh at myself as I was looking for inspiration—I struggled to find a topic that would inspire me to think and write, and there it was. Right before my eyes was my lesson on waiting patiently.

We are not a society that practices or values patience. We want it fast—instant gratification.

Notably, more tech-savvy people are used to getting what they need quickly. They and we get frustrated by what we deem wasting time idling by, waiting for our desires.

After my brief encounter on the ice, I started to think about the last time I patiently waited for a positive outcome. Was it in line at the lab? Not really. I recall checking my phone every minute. How about in the check-out line at the grocery store? I distinctly remember feeling annoyed by the slowness of the person in front of me.

When did "wait" become a bad four-letter word? What is our aversion to patience? Each of us has proven in our lives that waiting and letting things develop naturally have worked out for us before. Think about your first love, the first time you noticed each other and waited for the other to catch up. Were you waiting, staring at the phone, willing it to ring? These are the moments that have taught us patience. Each of these momentous life occurrences would have been missed if we jumped to the "end game" (the job, the relationship) before taking the slow discovery steps.

Many would claim the waiting is not worth it. But I bet you my fisherman would beg to differ. Rushing the process, he would miss the opportunity at success, the beauty of the eagles flying overhead, and the singing ice as Mother Nature serenaded him.

What have you been missing? It is in the waiting and the practice of patience that real learning happens. You are being asked to stop and listen.

Notice your feelings and those of the people around you. This is not something to be feared. It is something to be embraced. But should we wait forever? The fisherman is not going to sit for hours without a bite. Even a passionate sportsman knows when it is time to give up. We need to set a limit and decide how long is long enough before we pack up and move on.

Failing to move on will only lead to a place of constant desire with little fulfillment. In a sense, when we wait forever, we don't know what we are waiting for, or we are waiting for something that is not realistic.

The famous quote "Good things come to those who wait" comes to mind. I am the first person to admit that the time between action and resolution terrifies me. I like a plan, and I like when the plan goes according to plan. And I like my plan to happen in my time frame. Maybe that works in movies, but it is not suitable for real life. I believe many of our disappointments come from losing our patience and giving up too soon or getting stuck in the waiting mode spinning our wheels.

I have heard many young people say, "I went to school to be a (insert job), but I can't find a job." Should they give up their dreams and find a plan B, or should they stick it out and wait? I see this dilemma as a scale. It would help if you weighed the options of waiting and letting go. Unfortunately, our scale does not always allow enough time to see both sides equally. Neither should be rushed into.

We can all take a lesson from our joyful fisherman. The rewards for patience can be significant. It does not matter if the result you are looking for is a job, a relationship, or an opportunity. But at the same time, have an endpoint.

Be like the fisherman and come back another day with a new mindset.

I'm not falling behind or running late
(Wait for it, wait for it, wait for it, wait for it)
I'm not standing still
I am lying in Wait (Wait, wait, wait)
Lin-Manuel Miranda

Foundations

Have you ever had the experience when a word or phrase seems to be appearing everywhere you look: on the news, in conversation, at work? Well, for me, that word was foundation. A house collapsed during construction. The cause of the accident? A weak first floor. While advising a twenty-four-year-old negotiating the dating world, I advised, "no relationship, whether friend or lover, will work without a good strong foundation." Then, teaching my class the writing process, I found myself comparing the thesis to a solid foundation. You cannot build your ideas without it. Finally, my son is getting married next year. I recently told him that one of the most important aspects of a successful marriage is those few years when you are building a foundation.

There is a term for this, the Daader Meinhof phenomenon. "This phenomenon occurs when the thing you've just noticed, experienced, or been told about suddenly crops up constantly. It gives you the feeling that out of nowhere, pretty much everyone and their cousin are talking about the subject—or that it is swiftly surrounding you. And you're not crazy; you see it more. But the thing is, of course, that's because you're noticing it more [Zwicky]." After some thought, I decided that even though the phenomenon is not the universe necessarily talking to me, it might be worth it to examine why "foundation" is not leaving my mind.

The foundation of any relationship can be compared to the roots of a tree. At first, when the roots are shallow with little to hold on to, the tree is fragile and easily damaged. Think about a sapling that can be uprooted in a strong wind. But once the tree's roots begin to expand and grow deeper, this tree can withstand storms and bear fruit. So, if your relationship continues to exist at only the surface level, it will be damaged as soon as trouble brews. But if you continue to nurture the roots and give them room to spread, the basis of your relationships can withstand the twists and turns that are your life together.

I have been reminded of a clear example of a deep-rooted friendship recently. I spent a few days with a friend that I made when I was one year old. Well, maybe we weren't exactly friends then, but as soon as we could walk across our backyards, our relationship was sealed. That was over fifty years ago. Although we spent the beginning of our time reminiscing on our shared past (the depth of our old roots), we soon moved to the topics that consume most adults: children, college, jobs, marriage, and life. Sitting under the stars, sharing our deepest emotions, listening, and laughing like children, I was pleasantly surprised to notice our conversations were as comfortable and comforting as I remember them being when I was young. Our foundation that once brought our younger selves together had expanded to encompass our new selves. The roots have grown more profound, and our trees continued to flourish and beautify the world.

If you marry your best friend, you can take everything you know about friendship and multiply it by 100, factor in that you now live with each other. It's a wonder you need a solid foundation to survive. My husband and I have built our relationship based on shared ideas and true friendship over more than a quarter-century. We have lived together through parenting, family, friends, loss, and personal and professional successes. Our roots are strong, deep, and intertwined.

But many find themselves struggling to lay down roots, missing those deep connections. For some, we grow accustomed to being together and forget that all living things need room and support to grow.

I am not a therapist or relationship expert, but I am a communication expert and a people watcher. So, here's a suggestion that you might try to improve your relationship through better communication.

Before you invest time and energy into a complicated solution, take a few moments, and list the qualities that drew you to that person in the first place. Chances are, those qualities are still there even if buried under years of behavior. A compassionate human will remain compassionate; maybe they have just hardened with the pressures of work, marriage, and family responsibilities. Your job is to bring to the surface those feelings again. Take out the proverbial shovel and dig beneath the surface. Don't stop at the rote, "How was your day?" Stop. Listen. Ask the questions and hear the answers. Follow up appropriately with genuine concern or support. We get so used to phoning it in; we don't even realize that we have stopped listening and taking an active role in the partnership.

The key is not so much in the talking but the listening. I am not talking about the biological process of hearing. I am referring to the listening that happens when you hear the words, the body movement, and the silence. Listen to the content and discern the intent. What we say and what we mean can be completely different.

Which one are you hearing?

Here are some quick tips to become a better listener:

- Listen for more than just the words.
- What is being said between the words? In the Pauses? (Intent)
- What are the eyes and face telling us? Watch the space between the eyes for comfort/discomfort.
- Be aware of what your face and eyes are saying? (intent)
- Get in the habit of essential paraphrasing points back to your friend/ spouse. Say, "So just for clarity, you said...."

Every tree needs sunshine and water to grow. Like the tree, our relationships need to be nurtured for our roots to spread. Find the ingredients you are missing: love, nourishment for your soul, or maybe a deep connection. Or celebrate the fact that your roots are strong and healthy. Either way, remember to be an active member of your relationships. The rewards are worth the effort.

Zwicky, Arnold. "Just Between Dr. Language and I." The University of Pennsylvania. Aug. 7, 2005. (Jan. 21, 2015) http://itre.cis.upenn.edu/~myl/languagelog/archives/002386.html

Find Your limit - Then Crush It

If someone asked me for some humble life advice, my answer would be, "Each day allows you to make a choice. Do you let pain, illness, depression, stress of any kind win, or do you decide to be your best self, jump out of bed, and face the world with a smile?" I choose the latter. With a conscious decision to keep going, we are showing our fears who is boss. We are taking back control of our minds and bodies. I try to live my advice daily.

So yesterday, I chose to spend a chunk of the day walking across the Mario Cuomo Bridge, the baby brother to the George Washington Bridge, crossing the Hudson River slightly upstate for those not in New York. The entire walk up and back took about two hours and was 7.2 miles long. Facing a solid wind, chilly weather, and a disorienting bridge design with no clear horizon in sight, this was going to be an uphill climb, both literally and figuratively speaking. Yet, despite how my body was feeling, I felt the need to challenge myself.

Halfway through, I stopped to call my son. He asked, "Why did you do the whole thing? Why not walk just half. I think 3.6 miles is enough." My response was, "Could you eat half a bag of chips and not finish it?" Of course not.

I look at my life and see two stages, my younger self and who I am now. I had an everyday life where I could ask my body for something and respond accordingly. I was the active cheerleader and outdoorsy girl, and later an active

Mom. But for the past ten or so years, with a daily battle against arthritis, I have found myself reaching and trying things that literally throw me out of my comfort zone, transforming me into a competitor, fighting back against my body's wishes. The fight is physical and requires me to push myself in new ways. I have walked the Avon 39 in NYC, kayaked 5 miles to the ocean, and rode my bike 20 miles with my son. While physically demanding, each of these events was so much more than a fitness challenge or pursuit of bragging rights. For me, each was a personal exercise in self-discipline and mind control. I remember after the Avon 39, someone asked me what it was like. I recall saying it was more a brain than a body thing. When the body is ready to quit, you need to dig deeply into your mind to find the drive. The last few miles were about playing head-games to help me ignore what my body was screaming. Not surprisingly, I felt like a completely different person at the end of that day.

For me, a physical challenge is my body's reminder that I have a choice in my mindset. What I mean is, at some point during each of these challenges, the body sends signals to stop: shaking limbs, ragged breath, even pain, but your mind is what has to keep you in the game. No amount of weight and cardio training is going to prepare you for this.

It seems like our brain has a default switch that returns to that comfortable, safe space if we allow it to. I quickly figured out that this mental aerobics is not something you should do only once. Only practice and repetition will make this decision-making process more reflective and easier to access. Left to its own devices, our brain reverts to familiar patterns, and it convinces us that when things look too tough, we succumb to the body's desire to quit. Can you do one more mile? Can you finish the ride? If we let our bodies decide for us, we surely will not be as successful. When you find that inner strength, the good news is that a physical high happens with each small and not-so-small victory. This surge of positivity makes me feel strong, in control, and powerful. I know what you're thinking. I know my limits, and I am happy living in them.

Let's imagine for a minute what it would feel like to cross a finish line or reach a mountain peak; awesome, accomplished, alive! In contrast, how can we be happy with the comfortable?

Maybe you have never been athletic, learned an instrument, or written a book and think it is too late to start. Perhaps you find excuses from work, parenthood, or children. You can be sure if you need an excuse to "not do," you don't have to look too far. But how do you know what you are capable of if you do not push?

Ok, maybe an excessive physical challenge is not yet part of your everyday. Start with the small stuff. Make a list of all the things you wish you could do, a bucket list of sorts. But these are things that can actually be achieved. Let your imagination flow and be super creative. Just writing down a challenge should not be the scary part. Then pick one. Plan it. Do it.

You may never see me jump out of a plane or scale a mountain, as heights make me nervous, but I will continue to find ways to face new challenges and relish my success. I will continue to wake up grateful to write my own story every day and choose to give the world the best version of myself.

The art of going beyond small talk: Moving from social niceties to more in-depth conversation.

We are an efficiency-based country. Outside of our circle, we view communication merely as transactional. If there is nothing to be gained, then why engage? Most of us go through life with blinders on. We move from place to place, eyes down or headphones in, trying hard to avoid strangers, interaction, and any conversation besides the small talk that is impersonal yet extremely common. Almost as a default, we smile and ask strangers, "How are you?" We want and expect to hear "Fine," ending the interaction without any real feelings or emotions.

Yet, I am one of those people who enjoy non-transactional, vulnerable conversations with strangers. I love to get to that next level and learn about people, their likes, beliefs, and desires. In the grocery line, at the mall, a server in a restaurant. You make eye contact with me, and I can offer a witty comment or an invitation to engage. My children hate it. They always tell me to mind my own business, yet I am continually ignoring their suggestions.

Recently, I was forced to wait in a two-hour voting line in the pouring rain. The stress and tension of the event were palpable. I could have easily kept to myself like the other people waiting, gazing stoically off in the distance or staring at the ground, trying not to make eye contact with anyone, but that is just not who I am; I searched my general area to find someone that I thought looked open to talk with me. Two hours is a long time to be silent. Fortunately, right in front of me stood a fifty-something gentleman. His hands were encrusted with dirt, his clothes were dirty, and I noticed the other people around me were giving him a wide birth. I could hear my husband saying, "Ignore him." And my son adding, "He is minding his own business." I, however, saw the opportunity to try and make a new friend.

Just as I was thinking of some witty icebreaker, he said, "Wouldn't it be funny if we get to the front only to have someone tell us we are on the wrong line?" That is precisely the kind of conversation starter I would have used. This was fate, a like-minded man with an invitation to spend the next few hours in conversation. And boy, was I glad I did. This man was well read and knowledgeable on topics ranging from literature to comic books. Our talk was spirited, funny, and heartwarming, and then we reached the front of the line and went our separate ways.

For most, this brief interaction is a waste of time and energy. I will probably never see this man again, so there was no chance that our encounter would lead to a deeper relationship. But to me, it was a lesson in the power of learning from strangers and a simple acknowledgment and appreciation for the humanity of another. Given the state of the world, perhaps we'd be doing better if we actually engaged and tried to get to know each other a bit more. So, I left with new ideas, some interesting perspectives on old ideas, and a few book titles.

Maybe the fear of a more profound connection comes from thinking we have nothing worth offering or that we will be seen as a nuisance. This is a learned behavior that can probably be traced back to your childhood. Did a teacher say, "You aren't adding anything," were you bullied, did your parents put performance over praise? Without realizing it, these moments have a substantial effect on your adult self. Fortunately, the mind has the power to put things into perspective, and you can tell yourself that you are not the same person you were then. You have thoughts and opinions that are worth sharing. Share them.

For people who think they have something to say but are too shy to share it, their hesitation could result from embarrassment from not knowing what to say or blurting out something stupid. Ask yourself, "What is the worst thing that can happen?" Trust me. I have had my share of people look at me strangely and hurriedly walk away. Yet, these isolated instances have not dissuaded me from trying again. I am nothing if not persistent, and history has shown me that the effort is worth the reward.

Perhaps hesitation stems from our ever-present fear of the unknown. You also never know what baggage someone is carrying that might prevent them from seeming open or even rebuff your approach. And it could be fair. We look at all the terrible news every day as proof that our fears are well founded. But you deny yourself a chance to learn and grow each time you erect a wall between you and a potential new friend.

My experience reminded me that there are many good reasons to engage with new people, the most important being a willingness to explore a connection, leading to a deeper trust. Start small with the most practical idea, like a favorite restaurant or movie. I am not saying we need to jump into our deepest thoughts. Instead, dip your toe into the trust realm and slowly wade into a more intense sharing of ideas.

We need to learn to be open and trusting in the most non-threatening way. No one's life was dramatically altered by engaging in banter with a stranger. But it could be the foundation for deeper connections or friendship. It is an opportunity to make a first impression, and we all know, "you only get one chance to make a good first impression," so why not get in a bit of practice?

Humans are herd animals that crave connection with others. But if we continue to limit our circle to only those we know, our connections can get old and stale. Think about our Instagram or Facebook feeds. Social media is an echo chamber designed to reinforce your own beliefs. That is one of the reasons so many people rely on it. But how many times can we talk about the same topics with the same people? Where is the opportunity to practice our opening lines, work on our witty banter or partake in some verbal volleying?

We need to break the cycle that exists and take responsibility for teaching others the importance of connections. I remember telling my children when they were young, "Do not talk to strangers." For some people, they carry this childhood lesson deep into their adulthood. It is not supposed to be like that. Once we mature and can discern danger, we need to be able to engage with the world. Ignoring these brief social opportunities are missing out on creating connections and enhancing their lives. Simply think of this instead, if you don't talk to strangers, you could be missing out on meeting your new best friend, business partner, or love of your life. So what are you waiting for?

Let's Get Lost

I am a walker. Any time I can grab my sneakers and head out is the right time for me. I even put my walks into my calendar like I would for an appointment. They carry equal weight to life's other obligations. So, I was excited when the town's talk was a new hiking trail opening up near my house. So, of course, we (everybody should have a walking buddy) needed to check it out. We parked in the lot the first time and entered a well-marked gate, which dropped you on a paved path alongside train tracks. The walk followed the old railroad cutting through mountainous terrain. It was isolated and quite breathtaking. So beautiful, in fact, we wanted to go farther than our four-mile plan would allow. Staring off into the distance, you could see what appeared to be miles and miles of tracks ahead of us. It was like a scene from a movie where the leading man heads out on an adventure as the audience cheers him on. After this first excursion on the trail, I needed to determine where the twists and turns would lead. I knew that I could not walk the entire twenty-two miles, but I needed to see more. Fortunately, I found another entrance about two miles from the start. This one was a little less visible and took you through a short path in the woods to get on the trail. The trail was quickly within reach; we securely set off into the woods on our next walk.

It is incredible to me that a simple change of scenery brings up all kinds of emotions. Amidst the wooded area, the sun was instantly hidden behind the trees creating a dusky, closed-in feeling. I found myself checking that I had phone service just in case. The minute I sense insecurity, knowing I am not alone is an anxiety buster for me. With my friend's sense of direction and my phone in hand, I knew we could call for help. I could also map the distance to be armed with that knowledge for when we returned.

After about an hour and a few twists and turns, we found ourselves slightly disorientated. "I don't remember this being so far. Are you sure we went the right way at that last bend?" These were the questions running through my head and occasionally out of my mouth. As we moved deeper into the woods, I felt an inkling of anxiety starting to creep up the back of my throat. You know the feeling. Your skin starts to tingle, your heart rate speeds up, and worst-case scenarios race through your mind. I felt lost, unsure of myself, scared. Yet, I was only about three-tenths of a mile off the street. I could not pinpoint where these feelings came from, but they felt genuine.

Seeing my phone service fade away, I was grasping for control. I sent my friend to walk ahead of me. First, I was hoping she knew the way, and second, I needed a chance to compose or recompose myself. So I turned to my coping mantras: Slow deep breaths. You are safe. You are strong. You got this.

After a short while later, we were still in the thick of what I would consider the desolate woods following a path, or at least we hoped it was a path. With the trees down, it wasn't easy to discern one path from the next. At times, we had to choose to go left or right. Robert Frost's poem, "The Road Not Taken" was on repeat in my brain. Would a choice make all the difference? I sure hoped so.

Finally, we started to see water on our right. Even though we ultimately needed the water on our left, I took it as a sign. We had to be going in the correct direction. A little bit of weight lifted off of my shoulders.

Then it happened.

Feeling slightly less anxious, I yelled out, "Stop!"

My friend came to such an abrupt halt; I almost slammed into her back. She looked at me with concern. "Was something wrong?"

"No, something was right." We just paused, and without saying a word, she knew what I needed to do. Listen.

We stood silently, listening to the leaves flitting down from the trees. They made an actual sound as they cut through the air. The breeze bending the branches was speaking to me. And from the right, off in the distance, the water slapping the shoreline had almost a mesmerizing melody.

What was I afraid of? If I had not pushed through my anxiety, I would have missed out on this idyllic scene. I would never have had that moment of connection. Yes, we didn't know exactly where we were, but I felt like we just slipped through the magic wardrobe and found another world. This one was calm, peaceful.

My anxiety lifted like a fog at dawn. I did not look at my phone to check my email or watch to tell me where I needed to be. I was exactly where I needed to be at the exact time. No one wanted or needed anything from me.

I have never been one to let go of my controlling nature, but I permitted myself to be at that moment. I glanced down at the tattoo gracing my wrist, and those words stared back at me, "Just Be." When I first got it, these words were a reminder that I cannot fill the role of all things. You can finish the thought with just about any word that works at that moment: be quiet, be thankful, just be loved. Sometimes you have to pause and regroup, let someone else take control.

Our walk that day reminded me that we could use the outside world's beauty to help us look inward. On that chilly fall morning, I found a connection with the natural world, and I found happiness. As Ralph Waldo Emerson said, "Nobody can bring you peace but yourself."

Don't Be a Leader

From a very minimalistic perspective, we can say that there are two kinds of people in the world: leaders and followers. We all want to find ourselves in the first group, for we have been told that leaders exhibit the admirable qualities of strength of conviction, clear communication, and strategic problem-solving. Once you have mastered these skills, the sky is the limit on what you can achieve. Each of us reaches adulthood, aware that the desire to be leaders should be our goal. I recall broaching the subject when my children were about age ten, "Don't jump off the bridge; because your friends are doing it." Be the person walking to the other side. I hoped my subtle message would resound in them.

But these same traits that are admired, also drive some of us to be overly prideful and unwilling to ask for help. We often tell ourselves things like, "If (they) would just let me at it, I know I can fix the problem." Yet, a short time ago, I had to face the hard truth that there are things that I cannot fix, and that is an incredibly humbling experience.

Recently, my dad had fallen ill with COVID-19, a terrifying thing to hear during a pandemic, more so when your father is eighty years old. While his prognosis was good, the fact that I could do absolutely nothing to help him rendered me paralyzed by fear. I found myself checking for updates on my phone every five minutes. I was obsessed with the news, even when I did not want to hear it. My initial reaction was that there had to be some way

Judy Marano

to make this better, but I had very little to offer in this situation. So, what did I do? I worried. And while he has since recovered, the worry and deep sense of failure have not been resolved.

I remember hearing in church years ago that worry is a useless emotion because it takes away your focus from the task at hand. They even came up with a fun rhyme, "Don't get stressed, get blessed." This is even validated in science as stated in *Psychology Today*, "Worry adds nothing to preparedness, but it does add excess emotional baggage that, ironically, can heighten anxiety and interfere with your ability to function at your best." The fact of the matter is, that my worry is not going to change the reality. Now I must point out that worry or anxiety over a legitimate concern is warranted, but my problem was that I still did not feel better once the stress was resolved. I experienced general anxiety because I felt that my strong, independent thinker identity was failing me.

In a moment of clarity, I reevaluated my leadership traits and realized that they could help. I needed to step aside and let those who were much more qualified to take the lead. I cannot solve the problem; I am not a doctor or a scientist, but I can communicate effectively. More importantly, I can use my convictions and attitude to try to bring moments of joy to my dad and family. I can draw on my sense of humor to make them laugh. As they say, "Laughter is the best medicine." I can stay positive and share that positivity with my family and others in similar situations. Finally, I can educate myself because through education, fear has no power.

Being a leader is not only for the office or classroom. These are not merely a set of traits to become successful. Leadership is a fluid trait. At times it is magnanimous, and at times it's quiet. Knowing when to lead and when to follow, says Greg Shea, a faculty associate of the Center of Leadership and Change Management at Wharton, "You need a strong sense of who you are and what you do well. When you're aware of your limitations, you can surround yourself with people who are exceptional at what you're not."

Life is going to continue to throw challenges at us that are entirely out of our control. Today it might be a sick parent, a job commitment keeping you away from something you want to do, or even a pandemic. Two things happen when we are unable to gain control. The first is an overwhelming sense of disorientation and maybe fear because, as a leader, we are like a fish out of water. History has shown us that we know that the potential consequences have been weighed when we make decisions. The second accepts that we need to let someone else drive, even if only briefly. They are hopefully/probably more prepared. Ultimately, that will lead to a better outcome. Take a look at your life during these challenging times and decide that the best thing to do is lead when appropriate, but let someone else guide you when necessary.

https://www.psychologytoday.com/us/blog/the-minute-therapist/201703/worry-and-guilt-the-useless-emotions
https://executiveeducation.wharton.upenn.edu/thought-leadership/wharton-at-work/2012/09/know-when-to-follow/

The Art of Walking in Someone's Shoes

The universe is a persistent teacher. She throws us lessons repeatedly until we incorporate them into our daily lives. This muscle memory is akin to repeating a dance step over and over until we find ourselves moving automatically to the music.

Then the music changes, and we must pivot to stay standing. Of course, some of us are better at that than others.

I want to say that I consider myself a fixer. You know what I mean. Every family has one, along with the mediator, the cheerleader, and the thinker. I love looking at a problem from all sides and coming up with the best options. I would also consider myself a good listener. Years of teaching have taught me that listening and really hearing is when the most is learned. Combine these two skills, and I will get people gravitating towards me. In most cases, years of experience have provided me with the knowledge to respond to each situation appropriately. When presented with a challenge, I dig deep into my well-honed box of life tools, find the right solution and get to work.

However, I was recently thrown not one but two curveballs that reminded me that the universe is still teaching me vital lessons.

First, a close friend shared that she had received a diagnosis of suspected ovarian cancer. We met before her surgery to walk. She talked. I was shocked at the calmness with which she told me about her previous few weeks and the surgery plans. When I commented on her grace, she said, "It's so different when it is happening to your body." As much as I could, I tried to offer supportive words, but what could I say? I was not, nor have I ever been, in her shoes, so words like "I can imagine" or "I don't know what I would do" seemed shallow and fake. So instead of offering platitudes, I just listened. I responded when appropriate, but more importantly, I gave her space to share her feelings without judgment.

None of the tools in my box were at all helpful. Thank you, Universe, for the lesson. Here I thought I had everything I needed stored up in my 50+ years of life.

Clearly, I needed to pay attention because I sensed that this was not a one-time-only thing.

A few weeks later, one of my students disclosed that she was the victim of domestic violence. She told me she was stuck because she did not have any place to go with her two children. Then there was the issue of safety. I wasn't sure what I could do, but as a fellow woman, indeed, I would surely find something in my toolbox.

But once again, each solution I reached for did not fit the situation. I had no idea what this woman was going through. My own experience and personal opinions offered little for me to draw upon.

I have always had the fortune of having a secure roof over my head and food on the table. How could I possibly understand the fear of not having these basic human needs for myself or my children? Unfortunately, her shoes did not fit me.

I know there are policies for these situations, which I did later follow, but first, I realized that this woman needed a voice and a place to be heard. Whether her choice to tell me about her plight was conscious or unconscious, it was now my responsibility to react accordingly. I was honored that I was chosen, so I listened. She told her story. I listened. She told me about her kids, and I listened. Perhaps my presence brought her calm. I'm not sure, but I am sure we did build a trust that I intended to honor.

It is so easy to look at someone's situation and imagine what it would be like "if it were me." But both of my recent brushes with the unknown and uncomfortable have reminded me of the value of not needing to search for the right words and just support individuals during their experience.

But in these instances where words seem to fall short, how do you express that they matter to a friend or acquaintance? What can we say to show them they are heard? It's pretty simple. Terms like "I see" or "I understand" are enough. Another great tool is to repeat back what the person said to reaffirm that it matters. "So, you mean...." Or maybe just try a smile or a hug.

I love the saying "less is more." It is in times when someone you know is hurting that these words need to be your focus. It might be challenging to withhold your opinion or make suggestions. Let's face it, we all want to feel useful and valuable because our brain will reward us with a burst of dopamine, making us feel pleasure. But remember that part about walking in someone else's shoes? There are going to be plenty of times when you can't, and that is okay. The point of listening and caring is never about you—it's about connecting with that person with the issue. This connection requires attention and compassion. The best way to do this is to listen with your heart and your head.

In our daily conversations with coworkers, friends, and family, we are always expected to know the correct answer or have the right thing to say. Our jobs and our relationships depend on it. But since we are ever-evolving humans, we will come upon situations where we don't have the words. It is like dancing to music you have never heard before. The unknown can be scary, but if we stop and listen, we will find our rhythm and the steps to join the dance.

The Circle of Life

I was lucky enough to be a stay-home mom when my children were tiny. I do not take for granted that I could spend twenty-four hours a day with my twins. While I relished the time home, the reality is, even though I was home all day, I was not playing, holding, cuddling my children the whole time. That would be impossible unless you wanted the house as you knew it to fall apart around you. If you think about it, what matters is not the time spent but the quality of that time. I had plenty of time with my children, and though the working moms I knew had fewer hours at home during the day with their children, I observed that they made that time before and after work count. They took advantage of their time and made it count. I would even venture to say that hour for an hour; we probably spent the same amount of quality time with our children. Let's focus on that quality time.

During the early years, the impetus of quality times is mainly the parents. We decide when and what the activity should be. But if you are keeping score, the scheduling of the quality time rests solely with you—100% effort.

When children enter school, they are aware enough to realize that they can decide (in some cases) whether they want to spend time with us. Sometimes a child will even ask their parents to do something together. And boy, does that make us feel like wonderful, wanted parents. As a matter of fact, we brag to our friends about the times our children want to initiate activities.

We don't talk about the rest of the day. In my humble opinion, the dynamic moves slightly 90% us to 10% them.

Then there is another shift, this one more profound than the last. After college, children begin their own lives by finding time for their work, friends, and parents. Not by accident is family last. We can ask, but the reality is, based on geography, socioeconomics, and demographics, we have less control over the time spent together, so we learn to be patient and wait for an opening or an invitation. The good news is that time is mutually rewarding as you are now equal parts parent and friend. This moment in time is where my children are right now, and I value, relish, enjoy every moment that we spend together, albeit not nearly enough for my liking. Another change, 30% us-70% them.

As life continues and your children marry and have children of their own, the change in quality time is expected but still hard to get used to. Now they are initiating most of the time having the kids spend time with the grandparents while waiting for those small openings to invite a quality interaction: Us 40%, them 60%. Now that my children are grown, and the raising part is mere memories, we can interact as adults; both parties are equal, 50%-50%. I think of my mom and me.

We both initiate visits. We want to spend time together, and our conversations are thoughtful and mutually rewarding. We find ourselves sharing laughter and asking for advice. What better way to negotiate your life successfully than to ask the one person who not only has been there and done it but has done it with grace. We want to believe that this relationship will stay that way forever. None of us want to think about our parents getting old.

But the earth keeps rotating and time continues to move on. The cycle of life and changing connection became clear one day while walking by the reservoir. A car pulled up, and an older gentleman meandered out and headed for the waterline. He was followed by a 50-something son quickly exiting the car and grabbing two chairs and two fishing rods from the back of the car.

I said, "Great day for fishing." He responded with," I take my father here every three weeks, to this exact spot. "Their Spot," he called it. There, they sit, talk, "feed worms to the fish," and enjoy each other's company for a couple of hours. His story filled me with such joy. I quickly thought of the places that I could say are "our spots" with my mom and dad. I was pleased that a few spots jumped quickly to mind.

The effort for connection has made its final shift. Let's call it children 70%–parents 30%. We find ourselves relying on our children to care for, entertainment and support us. There is something so beautiful about children caring for their elderly parents.

Aging is inevitable. As such, there will come the point where we, as parents, require more and more care, and the final stage of our relationships with our children will, hopefully, involve 100% effort from our children. There is a beautiful circularity in this experience, something that is unique to humans. While aging is feared here in the west, we can look at how other cultures revere their elderly. These precious family members live with their children and extended family and are seen as the voice of the family. Their life knowledge and opinions are respected and honored, even while their bodies age and weaken. I am not implying that we must shift western society to the filial piety seen in other parts of the world. However, recognizing and accepting the cyclical nature of the relationship between parent and child will help come to terms with the fact that the give and take of relational effort must change. It is expected, it is healthy, and it is part of the circle of life.

Rusted and Waiting

My mother-in-law passed away earlier this year, leaving behind a house full of treasures collected over 80 years. So the big question was what to save? Do you keep what is useful, or do you stick with the things that have memories attached to them?

My husband and his brothers had the arduous task of sifting through her life and determining the value of each and every item. The brothers used the sticky pad method of marking things they wanted. Some homeless items found their way to outstanding outreach programs where they were welcomed with open arms. The rest, unfortunately, ended up in the dumpster. It is sad to think that someone's treasures can end up in the trash, but the reality is when someone dies, so does the connection to the things they owned.

Knowing that our house was already fully decorated, my husband was very discriminating about the items he brought home. Aside from a beautiful cabinet and two Queen-Anne chairs that I have admired for years, his haul primarily consisted of pictures and some random kitchen items. His brothers had a more challenging time separating the items from the memories, and our once empty barn is now the holding area for the things they wanted to save. As the house began to echo with emptiness, the carloads became less and less. On one of the final trips home, my husband brought two old rusted metal chairs and a small child's chair. I didn't ask why he took them, but him bringing them home spoke to their importance. I thought they were strange pieces to be attached to. But boy, was I wrong.

These metal chairs were constant companions in the backyard through his childhood. They were the chairs around the table during birthday parties with family. He recalled getting his first record album (Meatloaf's Bat Out of Hell) from a favorite cousin sitting in one of those chairs. For him, these chairs were reminders of those carefree childhood days when dinners outside and family BBQs were regular weekend events. Maybe they were the same chairs where he sat on a starry night with that first girlfriend or bonded with his buddies on a blustery fall evening? He didn't remember a time when the chairs were not in his life. Although he didn't know their origin, he claimed that they were older than his parents. I want to think that his parents inherited them from another family and another lifetime.

Clearly, they carried with them strong memories of years gone by. These white chairs were moved with his family from house to house and remained constant fixtures around the table, just waiting for a guest to stop, sit and enjoy the day. Even though you can clearly see the many years of paint on top of paint chipping away, I could appreciate their intricate design and the memories attached to them. You can look at them and think, "If these chairs could talk, they would have so much to say."

So it seemed fitting that they found their way, out from the cold dark basement left as garbage, to our backyard, where they are bathed in sunshine and happiness. This was their chance to start over, a chance to make new memories with a new generation. With a little bit of white paint, they look good as new. Do they match? No. But they have been relegated to the area around the garden where you can sit and read in the shade or for the audience to sit and cheer during a boisterous game of cornhole on a warm summer evening. When you sit in them, you can feel the history. You can almost smell the perfume of previous sitters, or maybe just the flowers adorning them. You can feel a connection to his past. If you listen very carefully, you can hear his mother happily laughing or telling him he is "being fresh." Her favorite saying.

You may be wondering about the third chair. The child's one.

This tiny child's chair matched the others. It sits about 18 inches from the ground with a seat big enough for a small child's bottom. When I asked him about it, the smile on his face was warm as his eyes turned inward as if trying to relive a memory. This chair, which was lost for a long time, was found hanging on a hook in the basement tucked away for safekeeping. It originally belonged to his grandmother, placed carefully next to an adult chair. He spent many a day with her because both his parents worked, and she conveniently lived down the street. This chair was his. He would spend time watching the squirrels with grandma. They would spend time outside just "talking." He remembers it being a quiet, peaceful time. The kind when you know you are loved and nothing else matters. This chair symbolized his childhood, so it only seemed fitting that since we do not have grandchildren (yet), we would use this chair as a place to put a pot of herbs. In their position, raised toward the sun, they can grow and nourish us just like the small chair did for him so many years ago.

Each of these chairs was picked not because they were pretty. As a matter of fact, his brother commented that "he took the strangest things." But they were not strange for him. It was a unique, important piece of the puzzle that was his childhood. We all have memories that make us smile. For some, these memories are attached to an item. What have you kept as a reminder of a simpler time? Maybe it's a blanket, a sweater, or even a postcard from a favorite vacation.

When we lose a family member, we want to hold on to as much as possible so that they remain present. But the reality is you don't need a bunch of stuff to keep a memory alive. You just need one or two items that will trigger many emotions and memories to pass onto future generations. So, when we receive guests at our beach house, we can tell the story of the chairs, and it is as if his mother is still with us, in the backyard, enjoying a beautiful sunny day.

It takes a Village

In over twenty years of teaching English as second language, my students have shared the hardships they experienced in their journeys, from surviving war and famine to being smuggled across borders and fleeing gang violence. Their stories inspire me and usually do not shock me anymore. But I was recently rendered speechless when a student told me that babysitters were not a thing in their community in South Africa. Instead, children as young as five or six would be left home alone to care for their younger siblings. The student said that children play outside all day, and the mother leaves meals to feed them. The neighbors in the tight-knit community watch each other's children as if they were their own. They are even free to discipline them. I was shocked. I immediately realized that I was trying to project my American views onto those of a completely different culture and practice.

The famous African proverb: "It takes a village to raise a child!" popularized by Hillary Clinton, originated from the Nigerian Igbo culture and the proverb "Oran a azu nwa." This same sentiment is repeated in many different African cultures, albeit with different terms. I had heard and used the phrase flippantly when I or someone I knew needed assistance. Even today, my mom often tells me I need a village to raise me. I used to take it as an insult that she did not think I could negotiate life independently. But that was because I did not fully understand what the saying meant and the fantastic benefits of having a village and knowing you need them.

Judy Marano

Let's use the analogy of making a quilt. Recently my sister, who was blessed with the artistic genes in the family, was making a quilt for a bridal shower. She previewed the different fabrics for me by placing each bolt of fabric in the order that would appear. At first glance, although it looked beautiful, I looked at the whole of the patterns instead of each one. My sister said that the way you arrange your materials is to find the dominant (boldest and brightest) color pattern and then find another piece of fabric that uses a similar color. At first glance, they might not seem to fit, but on further examination, they can enhance the quilt's richness, and you can see their value.

We should use the quilt image to build our village. Of course, our won't be exactly like the type you would find in Africa because villages are often tied together by religion, culture, and family. So, a village would inherently have similar ethical principles, more so than any friends. But our village will be built on similar values and beliefs. Choose people whose dominant traits brighten and deepen your own.

The result will be a beautiful complement of personalities and colors.

None of us is omniscient. We do not know what the future will hold and what particular mental and emotional trials you might encounter. So, the only way to stay afloat is to surround yourself with people who can fill in the gaps where you might falter. This is called social capital, the connections, shared values, and belief in society that allow people to trust each other and work together. I am not talking about the friend to run an errand for you or to pick up the kids; anyone can do that. I am talking about the people who stand by you, support you, and most importantly, are honest to a fault.

So let's start with how a village would have helped in raising our children. Each time you introduce a new person into your circle, this is an opportunity to bring in a new perspective or a new lesson learned. How much broader will our children's experiences be when they enter school if they had information from not just us. I admit that I thought I was a good mom. I exposed my children to their grandparents and my friends, allowing different opinions. But having them discipline my kids is where I drew the line. Mothers want that control that comes from establishing rules and order. I thought that was a mom-only job. How can I allow another person to take my place?

That is where I may have been wrong.

Another person might deal differently, but that can only open your child's eyes to the fact that each person does things a bit differently. Not wrong; just different. But thinking about it, taking direction and discipline from others better prepares them to enter the world. These kids will need to listen to diverse teachers, friends, and eventually even bosses throughout their lives. Being raised by many may make the transition from a sheltered home to the real world much smoother. Not only does your child need to see others, but parents also often benefit from an outside perspective. Your village with diverse backgrounds and cultural diversity adds color and richness to your family's world. Think of it as a painting. The primary colors come together to form the main image. These are your group of a small group of family or friends. They influence you and make you who you are. But the other colors that are added for accent trigger emotional responses or depth of understanding of the image. Each person's perspective can open doors to the person you might want to be. These colors and people challenge you. They hold you in check. They push you out of your comfort zone.

Although I try to surround myself with a diverse group of people, my village is so much more than a way to diversify my world. Marriage. Kids. Career. Life. It is hard. (There, I said it.) There is no way that I can successfully navigate it all. And the African proverb tells me that is a good thing. I am pretty capable alone, but taking a friend's offerings for help makes things easier.

Use the quilt strategy when building your life quilt, your village. Of course, you don't want all the people in your group to have the same attitude (colors). We can get consenting opinions from our social media. Sometimes, when we see a person, just like the material for a quilt, we look at the whole person instead of seeking out the part that makes them extraordinary. It is this dominant trait that will enhance your village and make it grow.

So, the next time someone uses the phrase, "It takes a village," don't think of it as a comment on your ability to survive alone, instead respond with, "Yes, it does, and isn't that wonderful?"

What we carry

You can learn so much about the human experience just by examining people in their daily lives. For example, take a seat by a window overlooking a busy street or visit an amusement park and put yourself on a bench. Just by watching, you will learn about people's habits and patterns, and as a result, valuable life lessons.

Recently, I was at the beach watching the parade of families make their way to the ocean. Each family was smiling as they joyfully strolled up the street, weighed down by their chairs, towels, coolers, games, books, electronics, and even a porta-potty for a toddler (you get the idea).

I was reminded of Mary Poppins and her magic purse from which she could pull just about anything a nanny or a child in her charge would need. She was never unprepared regardless of the situation and, so it seemed, neither were our families of beachgoers.

You need to ask yourself, what is absolutely necessary for a few hours? More importantly, what items can you live without?"

Maybe you are nervously laughing and saying, "I don't do that. I know how to relax unencumbered."

Okay, that may be true for you for vacations, but what about in your every day? Do you weigh yourself down with material things?

Our beachgoers happily carry their equipment to the beach, but then most likely realize that after a long day when the family is sunburned, tired, dehydrated, and swallowed half the ocean, their load feels so much heavier on the way home. What was supposed to enhance their day seems more like a burden now.

In the same way, what items are we dragging around every day that are weighing us down?

I am going to suggest that we unburden ourselves. Free yourself. Downsize your footprint.

This is harder than it sounds. I recall accidentally leaving my cell phone home one day not long ago, and I was so distracted by what I might be missing, I could not focus on the here and now. The uncomfortableness was akin to leaving home without your keys. It felt wrong. I felt lost. Then, throw a bit of control freak into the mix, and I spent the day creating terrible scenarios where I was incapable of helping family and friends who were indeed calling me asking for help. The fact is, when I got home, the only call or text was from a telemarketer that I probably would have declined anyway.

How did we become so connected to our stuff? We all want to feel important. We assign meaning to our things, whether as a status symbol or for sentimental reasons, and many are reluctant to give up the power or prestige garnered by having them.

I am not sure when the property became so crucial that it controlled our lives. When I was growing up in the '70s, we were a middle-class family in a small home. Although we were comfortable, we did not waste what we had nor look for extravagances. As children, we did not notice the name brands on our friends' sneakers or compare ourselves to others. After school and on weekends, we played in the street, rode our bikes to the park, or hung out at the neighbor's a few streets over. "Things" were not a thing. We moved and played and laughed. The only house rule was "Be home for dinner." And just like clockwork, we would arrive home at 5:30, wash up and be ready for 6:00 p.m. dinner. On the off chance that we were late, there was no way for our parents to contact us. My parent's call was a resounding scream for "Dinner!" out of the kitchen window. If you listened carefully, you could hear the voices of moms around the neighborhood, one by one calling their children home.

I recall feeling happy. Free.

I am going to take a lesson from my beachgoers. I have decided to work on being less weighed down and more like my childhood self. I have begun the process of lightening my load. I occasionally leave my cell phone home on purpose (and I feel like I am breaking some social law). After I pack a bag, I go back in and remove a couple of things I can do without. This transformation will not happen overnight, but with continual practice, I think I might be able to find that place where I have just what I need so that the trip home feels as light as the journey to my destination.

Acknowledgments

This book has been a labor of love that could not have been accomplished without some very special people. First, I want to thank my son, Jeffrey, for being the consummate editor. Even when I didn't want to admit it, he makes me a better writer. Also, his wife, Kelsey, for her much kinder edits. To Suzy Ranshousen, Phyllis Zand, and Ava Drutman, who were my readers and cheerleaders. I also want to thank my dear friend Carol Diebold, who was the sounding board for my ideas as we put miles and miles on our sneakers.

A very special thank you to Best Self Media for allowing me to publish some of these pieces in their online magazine.

Finally, to all of my family and friends who served as catalysts for my articles—each of you contributed in ways you can never imagine. I am grateful for the chance to share your and my stories with my readers.

Self-Love is not a dirty word

Motherhood teaches us that sometimes you need to put others first. If a friend asks for a favor, within reason, most of us will not hesitate to take the needed amount of time to put our tasks aside, no questions asked. The kids need new jeans? Off to the store you go rearranging your schedule. Your husband needs a hand trimming the brushes? You drop your plans for the day and grab your gardening gloves. We, as women, moms, wives, see these interruptions as part of our job. They are the moments we take out of our day to make someone else's life a bit easier. And for the most part, they make us feel wanted and needed.

When it comes to us and our wants and needs, these moments are put on the back burner for a more convenient time. Things are priorities when they involve others, yet they never make it to the top of the list when they are for us. I have heard moms say they never buy clothes for themselves anymore because things for the kids seem more essential when you attempt to go to the mall. There never seems to be enough time to do all the required stuff and still have time for a bit of self-love.

I don't recall ever being taught the importance of self-love, but my mom spoke loudly with her actions. I remember her meeting with a neighbor at least once a week to work on the month's craft. They would drop us in front of the TV or in the yard and spend a few hours creating projects, making candles, making Christmas ornaments, etc. She would also play tennis and bowl with friends. My mom did not feel bad, nor did she apologize for spending time filling her cup with her creativity. Instead, she said, *"You need time away from your everyday tasks as a way to survive the mundane."* Even before the phrase was coined, my mom knew the importance of self-love. I am a lucky girl who has taken these lessons and incorporated them into my life regularly.

I have never been the person who waits for an event to spend quality time on myself. I "treat" myself with a manicure when I get a new client. I take "me" out to lunch when I complete a new story. When I have completed my chores, I take a book and sit quietly, enjoying a story about a faraway place. No waiting, no excuses, pure self-indulgence. I have friends that comment on my taking what I need with things like, "I wish I could be like that." My response is always the same. "You can be? Start by loving yourself."

Why is it so hard to treat yourself lovingly? Sure, you give yourself the basics, food, water, shelter, and maybe even a chai latte on occasion. But really, we should be celebrating ourselves often. We are amazing women who sacrifice for others, hold jobs, are business owners, and still have time to be the go-to person for the family. But the idea of rewarding yourself even for the small stuff does not come naturally.

This may be a woman thing, but I know I have friends who dangle self-reward until they achieve something significant. Who deems what is significant? I decided we are terrible judges when the event pertains to us. For example, a friend of mine recently announced that she lost 25 lbs. Wow! What an accomplishment. But instead of celebrating, like I thought she should, she said, "I still have 30 more to go". No celebration here. I immediately broke into an explanation of self-love and the importance of rewarding even the tiny things. By rewarding yourself, you are acknowledging the steps so far and motivating yourself to continue. When you force yourself to wait for the big *ta-da*, you deny the small steps to getting there. Instead of the small gift being a distraction, it can act as a motivator. It can keep you focused and keep your eye on the goal.

Of course, there is another valuable benefit to self-love. I use a Happiness Journal that "requires" me to write one sentence about something that brought me joy over the course of a day. I do this every day, no matter what the universe throws at me. Although, I admit that some days my joy comes from merely waking up.

Let's be honest; some days stink. This is the perfect day to celebrate. The fact is, I need self-love more when the world deals me a bum hand. So, in the mindset of practice what you preach, after dinner, I grab my sneakers and head to a coffee shop for an iced chai latte. Does it make me feel better? Well, yes. At least I can go to sleep knowing that I took care of myself, and tomorrow will be a better day.